YO, LITTLE BROTHER VOLUME II

Basic Rules of Survival for Young African American Males

Anthony C. Davis
Jeffrey W. Jackson

Press Comments on *Yo' Little Brother, Volume II*

Chicago, Illinois

Second Edition, First Printing

Front cover illustration by Harold Carr

Copyright © 2006 by Anthony Davis and Jeffrey Jackson

Printed in the United States of America

10-Digit ISBN #: 1-934155-01-2
13-Digit ISBN #: 9 781934 155011

"This book provides much needed guidance and reinforcement."

Tonya Pendleton
The Philadelphia Daily News

"*Yo, Little Brother Volume I*...is aimed at helping young black males navigate the often hostile maze we call American culture."

Junius R. Stanton
The Black Suburban Journal

"With a blend of extensive factual research, a mix of interpersonal discovery, and told in a down-to-earth tone, *Yo, Little Brother Volume I* should be in every home, high school class, college dormitory and every concerned father's briefcase."

Michael J. Rochon
The Philadelphia Tribune

"*Yo, Little Brother* gives 'in-your-face' advice to help keep young men out of trouble."

Marcia Y. Mahan
Black Elegance Magazine

125095

"Davis and Jackson's new release is an excellent and much needed book of wisdom."

"A powerful tool for parents, educators, and anyone who associates or works with youth."

"The authors have a knowledge of the street that infuses the whole book."

"Finally! A book for young black men."

ACKNOWLEDGEMENTS

We would like to thank everyone involved with this labor of love. Once again, Dr. Kunjufu – thanks for giving us a national stage to share our ideas upon. Thank you again, Sandy Moore – your clerical and organizational skills are worth much more than we can pay you.

We want to say a prayer of gratitude for all of the people who helped our cause for "Yo, Little Brother" Volume II: Tonya Pendleton of the Philadelphia Daily News, the late Mike Rochan of the Philadelphia Tribune, Kelly Dutton and Dawn Jones of K&D Communications, Junius R. Stanton of the Black Suburban Journal, Vernon Odom of "Visions," the late Barbara Smith of "Community Journal," Kim Hall Jackson of KHJ Enterprises, Eleanor Jean Hendley of KYW-TV, the Reverend Fred Simpkins of Clear Voice Ministries in Sacramento, the staff of Hakim's Bookstore in West Philadelphia, Black Images Bookstore in Dallas, the Shrine of the Black Madonna in Houston, Lecia Warner of Basic Black Books in Philadelphia, Aisha Jackson of Hewlett-Packer, Delaware State University, Marvin Hargrove of Coca-Cola, the African American Museum in Philadelphia, Bynum Ventures, Intercultural Family Services, Inc., and Shively Willingham of the School District of Philadelphia.

TABLE OF CONTENTS

INTRODUCTION

Tony came up with the idea of a book of rules for young black men. As a teacher in a Philadelphia high school, there were many instances when an exasperated parent (often a single mother) or caretaker would ask, "What can I tell my son? I don't know what to say to this boy." In trying to provide something supportive, encouraging or instructive, he would often be reminded of things he had been told or had heard from numerous and varied sources.

Over the years, he compiled the tidbits, adages, observations and witticisms into 50 rules for black boys.

It was nearly ten years ago, in late 1995/early 1996, when Tony came to me and told me about his 50 rules for black boys. I was the director of a drug treatment center and partial hospital in North Philly, and had been a mental health treatment supervisor and administrator for several years.

Having been faithful friends since the first week of our freshman year at historically black college Hampton Institute more than twenty years earlier, Tony and I had intimate knowledge and understanding of each other's lives, families, neighborhood, and community experiences, and some of the personal experiences which had created our similar, but distinct perspectives.

We both grew up in the inner city in Philadelphia during the most violent era of street gang warfare. Our families had ensured that we had the best education possible and we were both communicators. We had both beaten the odds by making it to our forties without criminal records or jail time, drug habits, estranged or uncared for children, or financial disaster.

We had both been involved in the black power movement of the 60's and 70's, and were students and proponents of African history and culture, and African-centered thought. We were both spiritually grounded through our religious upbringing, and our study and discussion of world religions and spirituality. Tony felt that my family of origin (traditional nuclear family of four sons raised by an old school military dad) would provide a good counterbalance to his (only son of a single mom with two sisters, male and female cousins, aunt and grandmother).

Now, as mature family men who worked with young people in teaching and mental health, we felt we might have something to say that could help some young brothers; knowing as we did that only a psycho-educational process would provide the substance needed to help young black men understand and navigate the treacherous terrain that is faced by black men in today's society.

We set out to be myth busters who confronted and debunked certain stereotypes.

1. That black men don't care for or about, or take care of their own.
2. That young black men and the people who care about young black men don't read.

We wrote "You, Little Brother" for four reasons:

- As a guide for boys and young men to use in making decisions – many of which will have lasting impact on their lives.

- As a reference for caretakers and concerned persons who are not male or African American and who interact with young brothers, to have an idea of some of the peculiarities of the black male experience.

- As a way to speak directly to young brothers – man to younger man – and impart some of the important cultural mores. *OUR BOOK IS FOR YOUNG BLACK MEN, NOT ABOUT YOUNG BLACK MEN*.

- As a support and reinforcement for the vast majority, the teeming multitude of young black men in America and the world, who try hard to do the right thing and be good guys in the face of seemingly endless lies, bad mouthing and corruptive influences.

Stay strong and positive. We are one in unity and power. Peace and love.

– Jeffrey W. Jackson

Social Survival

Think Before You Tattoo

Doctors are making a whole lot of money from young people who want tattoos removed. Tattoo artists are also making extra money by covering up tattoos that are no longer wanted. All of this is happening because young folks don't think before they get tattooed.

Many young African Americans get permanent marks on their bodies without ever knowing what they mean. You see young brothers and sisters with Chinese symbols on their arms and they don't speak Chinese. How do they know they aren't giving the world the wrong message? One Chinese character could have many meanings.

If you choose someone that you consider a hero for your tattoo, be careful. Today's hero could be tomorrow's villain. How many athletes, movie stars and other celebrities end up as criminals? How many new designs become outdated? How many ideas go out of style? Will what you have now make you look like a fool years from now? Will that tattoo be used to identify you by the cops or a gang? Will it offend another person's beliefs?

Do your homework and think twice about something that will be on your body for life. You stand for whatever art you wear.

Drink Responsibly

When you turn 21, you will become a man in the eyes of the law. One of the privileges of being an adult is that you can legally purchase alcohol. Don't use this as a reason to go crazy.

In some colleges and other social circles, people celebrate their twenty-first birthday by going out and having twenty-one drinks. They either end up puking their guts out, having car accidents, or losing their drivers licenses because of drunk driving.

There is nothing wrong with having a drink or two if you are over twenty-one. There is a big difference between having a drink or two and being a fall-down drunk. We have to be very careful about drinking. We have too many drunks and winos in our communities already. We don't need any more.

A glass of wine with dinner is fine. A beer at the ball game is good for soothing a sore throat from cheering. A glass of champagne is good for toasting someone's wedding, birthday or anniversary. The problem comes in when we overdo it. Know what your limit is and stick to it. Make a rule that you will only have one or two drinks when you go out. Don't get sloppy drunk. Drink a glass of water with every drink. This will make you drink less and save you some money too.

Social Survival

If you feel tipsy, do not drive a car or operate any heavy machinery. You will only be putting yourself and others in danger.

Once you have reached your preset limit, don't let friends talk you into drinking any more. Friends may think they are making you have more fun, but real friends respect your wishes.

If you don't think that alcohol is destructive to our community, go to any prison. You will find that many convicts will tell you that they were drunk when they committed their crimes.

Never Leave Your Food or Drink Unattended

If you go to a dance or a party, never leave your glass or plate unattended. You never know what could happen to it while you are gone.

The newspapers carry stories everyday about someone who was slipped some drug or something while they weren't looking. There are many different things that someone could put in your food or drink to knock you unconscious, or make you trip.

Jeffrey Dahmer killed more than a dozen young men. Some of them he even ate. This sicko lured young men to his apartment to play video games. He offered them some soda to drink and they accepted. Before they knew it, they were waking up hog-tied and gagged. They could not get away or even scream. They were tortured, killed, cooked, and then eaten.

You see young girls on the evening news talking about how they were given the "date rape drug," and were taken advantage of.

There were rumors circulating for years about people losing body parts while being drugged. The rumor went something like this: A guy meets a beautiful woman at a bar. She tells him that she likes him and wants him to come back to her hotel room with her. She pours him a drink and promises him a good time. He wakes up the next day in a bathtub full of ice with a pain in his side. He notes that he has a long cut that has been stitched back up. He calls 9-1-1. When he is in the hospital, he is informed that his kidney was surgically removed.

Now, I don't know if this story is true or not. I do know that it could have been avoided if the guy hadn't taken that drink.

Don't Try to Live the Life of Movie Gangsters

Every rapper featured on Yo! MTV Cribs has a picture of Scarface somewhere in his home. The funny thing about Scarface is that he wasn't real. Black kids have Al Pacino plastered on their walls like he was a real-life hero.

This is only one example where we go overboard. Sure, there have always been gangster movies and T.V. shows. Your parents watched The Untouchables, The Godfather, and all kinds of movies with guys like James Cagney and Edward G. Robinson as thugs. The difference is that we did not try to emulate their lifestyles. We were able to separate reality from the fictional movie.

Posters of sports heroes and musicians are one thing. They at least give you a goal to shoot for. It's okay to want to throw a ball as far as your favorite quarterback. If you put his poster on your wall, perhaps his accomplishments are something you could shoot for. Wanting to attend the college of your favorite player is great motivation.

If you put up posters of black heroes, perhaps you could aspire to do something for your people and the world. Some have posters of their favorite entertainers. This is cool, but make sure that the entertainer you put on your wall is doing something positive for your community.

Social Survival

Some young brothers look to a fictional gangster as someone they want on their walls because they think Scarface was tough, and they think that having a Scarface poster will somehow make them look tough too.

This is the ultimate in self-hate. It reminds me of the statues near the Sports Complex in South Philadelphia. There are statues of Wilt Chamberlain, Mike Schmidt, Julius Erving, and Rocky Balboa. What's wrong with this picture?

The answer is that Chamberlain, Schmidt and Erving are All-star Hall of Famers, while Rocky did not exist. They were real people. Rocky was a movie.

With all of the great fighters to come out of Philadelphia, why doesn't one of them deserve a statue? The answer is that people can easily be brainwashed by what they see on a movie screen.

The World Doesn't Owe You Anything

If you go through life thinking that the world owes you something, you will be seriously disappointed. You get nothing from being born but life.

You have to work to eat. You have to toil to have a nice house or car. These things don't come to you. Too many young black folks think that all you have to do is get a rap album contract or join the NBA, and the world is theirs. This is a dream that will only be met by a handful of brothers a year. The millions of other young brothers need to think about earning a living some other way.

This is why so many young brothers turn to lives of crime. They see that they won't make their high school teams, let alone the NBA. They didn't pay attention in school, so now they are only qualified for very low-level jobs. They feel that the world owes them more. They see that the drug dealers make ten times the money that they make. They see easier money and they go after it.

The problem is that they only see the money. They don't see the violent side of holding down your drug turf. They don't see the pain of taking a bullet. They don't see getting locked up. They just see what they think the world owes them.

Social Survival

The world does not owe you money, an education, a good life, or love. The world does not owe you a house, a car, or a peaceful living condition. These are all things you have to earn or create.

Whenever you see another brother with something worth having, don't speculate on how he got it. Ask him how. If he is a legitimate brother, he will probably tell you that he got it through hard work, not because it was owed to him by birth.

You are Only as Good as Your Word

When you give your word, keep it. If you make a promise to do something, do it. If you make a promise to be somewhere, be there. If you make a promise to help someone, help them.

Always keep your word. Try not to let people down. Keep your word to your parents that you will study. Keep your word to your teachers that you will do your homework. Keep your word to debtors that you will pay your debts.

You are only as good as your word. When you take the driver's test, you give your word to the state that you will obey their laws. If you go to court, you give your word to tell the truth, the whole truth and nothing but the truth.

Many business deals are done on a basis of a handshake and a person's word. Many love relationships form on the basis of a word. Dental appointments and doctor's appointments are usually done on the approval of your word that you will be there on that time and date.

You give your word when you get a credit card. You give your word when you join fraternal organizations. You give your word when you tell someone sick or elderly that you will visit them. You give your word when you tell little kids that you will play with them. There are so many times when you will give your word during the course of a day. Make sure your word is bond.

Don't Exclude Brothers From Other Religions

When I was growing up in Catholic school, we were told that all other religions were false. We were told that our protestant friends, although Christian, were not practicing the true faith. We were told that only true Catholics were going to heaven. Those of us who questioned this idea were treated as if we had just committed a mortal sin.

We were basically being taught to be close-minded when it came to other religions, and that was wrong. I wondered if my protestant friends were being told the same thing. And what about my Muslim friends? Did the Iman tell them that none of us were going to heaven? If they did, they were wrong.

We have so many things that divide us as a people that we should not let religion be one of them. It wasn't only Christians who marched with Martin Luther King, and it wasn't only Muslims gathering with Minister Farrakhan at the Million Man March. Those brothers put religion aside in those situations, and they came together and shook up the world.

When people see you coming down the street, they don't see a Catholic, Protestant, Muslim or Jew. What they see is a black man. Celebrate weddings, funerals and all other religious and cultural events in the lives of the people that you know. Let religion become a unifying force, not a divisive one.

Never Harbor a Fugitive

I once let an old college friend and his family stay at my house for a week. He told me they needed a place to stay because their apartment was being repaired after a kitchen fire. Since he was cool with me, and I had a big, three-story house, I said okay. I hadn't seen him for a while, but I figured he was cool.

He came with his wife and three kids, whom I met for the first time. They stayed on my third floor. Actually, they stayed in one room on that floor because I was doing some work on the other two rooms.

The person who was showing me how to do the plastering was the father of a friend of mine. He told me that there was something suspicious about my friend. He wanted to know why my friend didn't stay with some of his own family since he was from the town that we lived in. His wife was also from our hometown . Didn't she have any relatives that she could stay with? I didn't give it much thought, but I should have.

Years later, I was watching America's Most Wanted on Fox T.V. and guess who I saw? It was my so-called buddy. It seems that he was on the run from the law for murder. He had killed one of his adopted children right before he had come to stay at my house. He introduced me to three kids when actually he had four counting the little girl that he murdered.

He knew all along that he was putting me in danger by staying at my house, but desperate people don't care about other people. He knew that if he had told me about what he had done I would not have let him stay at my house.

If you hide a friend of yours who is in trouble, you could likely end up in jail yourself. You could be charged with harboring a fugitive, obstructing justice, conspiracy, or a number of other offenses.

When your friends are on the run from the law, steer clear of them.

Body Language

If you don't think that body language counts, all you have to do is watch any one of the television court shows. Judge Judy demands that you look her square in the eyes while testifying. Judge Mathis will mock you if you appear to be speaking lazily or slouching. Judge Joe Brown will tell you to stand up straight, and you had better not roll your eyes at Judge Milian on The People's Court.

Sure, they are only T.V. judges, but there are times when you can learn something from TV. One of them is common sense body language.

Do you think that you could get away in public grabbing your crotch like Michael Jackson? I hope you have more common sense than that.

Do you think you can give thug looks to the cops like the rappers on the videos? Don't be crazy.

If you want to do poorly in school, sit in the back, slouch down in your seat, fold your arms, and look out the window. This will guarantee that the teacher feels you don't give a damn.

Sure, your mother always told you to stand up straight. She was right! Good posture makes you look confident. Napoleon was a bit over five feet tall, but in all of his portraits he stands like a giant. You can see that he is physically small, but you can still see that he's in charge.

Don't Pick Up Hitchhikers

Strangers on the road should stay strangers. When you get a car, remember that. You should never pick up a hitchhiker – especially at night.

Just because a person looks good is no reason to pick him or her up. You don't know who they are or where they are coming from. They could be carrying a gun and jack your car. They could be on the run from committing a crime. They could have a severely contagious disease. Anything could happen. You never know.

You don't really need another passenger to get to wherever you are going. All you are doing is putting yourself into a potentially dangerous situation.

There have been plenty of movies about what can happen when you pick up strangers and give them a rise. Have you ever seen the "Texas Chainsaw Massacre" or "The Hitcher?" These are just two examples of stories that begin with people picking up strangers on the road. They end in tragedy.

As a young black man, you could pick up someone who blames a crime on you. Who would really know if you were guilty or innocent? Someone could say you robbed or raped them. Then what?

So, what is the best way to pick up hitchhikers? There is none. Keep on driving.

Don't Bite the Hand That Feeds You

Beggars can't be choosers. If you live with your parents or someone else who buys the food, then there is no need for you to complain about what's on the table.

You shouldn't complain about someone's car if they are giving you a free ride. As long as you can get to where you need to go safely, then don't dog someone over their car.

When you complain about something that someone is doing for you for free, you burn bridges instead of building them.

The term for this is being ungrateful. I have seen students take one or two bites out of a free breakfast then throw the rest around the school. Then they complain later that the schools don't feed them well.

We have to learn to count our blessings. We have to learn to be thankful for what we have and grateful to those who provide for us.

You might complain that the rules in your parents' house are too strict. Meanwhile, you use their water, gas and electricity for free. You have a bed to sleep in, a roof over your head, a television, stereo, and probably a computer. If you have all of this, then you have no need to complain or speak poorly of those who provided them for you. If someone bails you out of a problem, you can't complain that it didn't happen sooner.

Call a Friend

When you feel that you want to do something rash, call up a sensible friend. No matter if this friend is a relative or not. It makes no difference if your friend is male or female. It doesn't matter if your friend is an old head or a young buck – just give them a call.

A good friend isn't afraid to tell you when you sound crazy. A good friend doesn't agree with everything that you say. A good friend doesn't want to see you fail. A good friend will tell you when you need to chill. A good friend will not only stand up and fight for you, but he will also try to keep you out of fights. A good friend will make you feel like you don't have anything to prove.

Don't rely on your friend's advice. You have to ultimately make your own decisions, but it always pays to share an idea with someone before you make big moves. They may provide a point of view that you haven't thought of. It can't hurt.

Let people know that you are alive. There is no excuse for you to not drop a line to an old friend. If you don't have a phone, send an e-mail. If you don't have a computer, write a letter. Everyone has a pen and a piece of paper. Now all you need is an envelope and a stamp.

Social Survival

You never know if your call can be just what your friend needs at a time of trouble. Life is a two-way street and you get what you give. What goes around comes around. One of the greatest things we have is our support of each other. So, call a friend, give some love and get some back.

Keep Your House Clean

One way to turn off potential girlfriends is to have a dirty house, apartment or room. Some girls might not care, but are those the girls you really want? Most girls would be flattered to know that you thought enough about them to clean up your place because they were coming for a visit.

People judge you by what your place looks like. You may not have the newest furniture or appliances, but if they are clean, it doesn't matter. You go into some people's houses and you can tell what they had for dinner for the last three days.

Let's face it! A dirty house is trifling. If your house is messy and disorganized, then you probably are too. Don't expect anyone else to have to clean up after you. It is your responsibility. Unless you have a butler or maid, then you need to get on the ball.

The fastest, easiest and cheapest way to improve your living conditions is to keep your place neat and clean. Something that is amazing is how great a difference removing grime like fingerprints, food marks, pencil marks, etc. makes on your doors, walls, tables and light switches. Get some cleanser or spray cleaner or other soap and clean up.

An old army saying goes, "If it moves, pick it up. If you can't pick it up, clean it. If you can't clean it, paint it."

Cleanliness is next to Godliness.

Know Your Neighbors

It is strange how some people can live in a neighborhood all of their lives and not really know anybody there. Some people in larger cities don't know their neighbors or people who live in their own apartment buildings. Some people like to live a life with little contact with neighbors, but the people who know their neighbors have more going for themselves.

Knowing the people next door or across the street could help keep your property from being burglarized. Neighbors can give you advice on goods and services that could save you time and money. People that you know will be more likely to call the cops if you are being mugged or assaulted.

You never know when you are going to need a ride or a tool or a babysitter or a job reference or directions somewhere or a book or a hand to help you lift something heavy.

Your neighbors are people who are an extension of your family. They are your close community. They will help you celebrate and they will help you mourn. Treat them with respect and love and your neighbors will love you back. Treat your neighbors the way that you want to be treated, and most of the time they will reciprocate.

Don't get me wrong! I'm not saying that you and your neighbors have to be best friends or bosom buddies. I'm not even saying that you have to like each other, but you need to know who your neighbors are. They need to know you too.

One of the best things about growing up in the 'hood in Philly was the way everyone had fun together at block parties, rec. centers and neighborhood pools. One way to increase the peace and stop the violence in our communities is to respect each other through knowing our neighbors.

Know How to Cook

When we hear young brothers say they can't cook, it bothers us. Black men have been on the forefront of cooking since the beginning of recorded history. Go downtown to just about any fancy restaurant and you have a good chance of seeing a brother in the kitchen.

We feel that if you can read you can cook. Most packaged foods come with directions on the box. Then there are hundreds of cookbooks written by black people that you could get recipes from. If you mess up, try again after you read the instructions again.

To be a black man and say that you can't cook is an insult to all of those brothers who raised their families by working as cooks on trains during the last century. Look at all of the Islamic brothers cooking at Muslim sandwich shops around the country. Go down to New Orleans and you will see that brothers are making all kinds of African, French and Creole dishes.

In Kansas City and Chicago, brothers will argue over who makes the best barbecue. Brothers in Virginia will make a ham that your taste buds will remember. Black men on both coasts and in the Gulf States are famous for church fish fries.

Let's face it. A brother who can cook for himself can take care of himself. He doesn't have to waste time waiting for someone to cook for him. He doesn't have to fall in love with the first girl who can cook well. He can provide for his family when they are hungry. He becomes more valuable to many social situations.

A brother who can't cook is a slap in the face to Uncle Ben, Famous Amos, and Chicken George. Knowing how to handle yourself in the kitchen is a good way to get a job too.

It's Okay to Cry

Most of the tough guys who think crying is for sissies have never been to jail. Ask any ex-con. He will tell you that a river of tears flows every night. Tough men, grown men, thugs all break down and cry at night. It may be triggered by memories. It may come as the result of loneliness. It might come from fear, depression, or any other problem that comes from being locked up.

Comedian Richard Pryor once said that he never got into a fight until after he cried, but once he started crying, "Look out!"

It is okay to cry. It is only an emotion that has no shame attached. A good cry cleanses the soul. A cry releases all of the pent up hostilities that can cause deadly stress.

In the classic Kung Fu movie, "Enter the Dragon," karate master Bruce Lee tells his young student that, "It's the emotional content" which is key to the success of the move he is practicing. Indeed, the emotional content of what we do determines whether an action or activity is good or meaningful, or just routine, humdrum, meaningless. So, it is good to recognize your emotions in the moment and embrace them.

Sometimes sad things make you cry. That's the way it is and that's the way it's supposed to be. Crying is your body's way of reacting to the emotion you are feeling sad or happy. It's natural and uncontrollable. Crying doesn't make you less of a man. It makes you more human.

Behind the Back

Don't waste time, energy or blood by worrying about what someone said behind your back. If they didn't say it to your face, then ignore it.

People find it easier to talk about someone when they are not there to defend themselves. This is actually the cowardly thing to do, so let them continue. Don't get involved in the back and forth of he said, she said. Let it rest. Those who want to talk will talk anyway. Don't get involved in that mess. It will make you look like a fool. It's been said that if a wise man argues with a fool, you can't tell the difference. Be stronger and wiser than that.

In years with the School District of Philadelphia, we have seen many fights that started over he said, she said. Most of the time, nothing was really said. Many times the person was lied to by one of their so-called "friends" who wanted to see a fight. You never know what was said about you unless it is said directly to your face. If someone wants to talk about you, but not to you, that's their problem. Don't make it yours.

Sticks and stones may break your bones, but words will never hurt you.

BSBSMGD – Be Safe, Be Smart, Make Good Decisions

Be Safe:

It might sound corny, but it can save your life. SAFETY FIRST!

None of your dreams can come true, nor your goals be reached, if you're not around. So, keeping safe and sound so you'll be around must always be your first priority. It goes all the way from the most basic: being careful crossing streets, using your street smarts to safe sexual practices, to avoiding risky activities and behaviors, and using proper safety equipment in the right way when playing.

Don't fall into the deadly traps of drugs and gangs, fast money, fast women, bling bling, and instant gratification. These things will hurt you in the long run.

Watch your back. Don't trust anybody farther than you can throw them. Be in charge of your own security every minute, every second, every hour, day and night, 24-7. Watch where you are going and who you hang with. Turn down that Walkman, C.D. player or I-Pod when you are walking or on public transportation. You want to be able to hear the world around you. Don't expect anybody to watch your back. You come into this world alone, and that is how you will leave.

Be Smart:

Fat Ed, Scooter, Mousie, and the rest of the Ant Hill Mob gang in South Philly called me Professor. It was a bust (term of ridicule), but also a term of respect. I wasn't in the gang, but because of my family and friends' connection and time in the hood, I didn't have to be in the gang. And since me and my boys were willing to take the gangsters on in any kind of sports competition (and put it to 'em hard), we were exempted from the gang war drafts. But we still had to deal with the gangers on an everyday individual basis.

Because education was stressed in my home, my Peabody glasses, briefcase, and use of proper grammar and enunciation led the local thugs to call me Professor. But it also showed a measure of recognition and respect from the jitterbugs and I learned to tolerate the name and accept the role that went with it.

I was surprised to hear from another friend later in the years that I was known around the neighborhood as being smart. He told me I would've been all right in jail because people would need reading and writing skills and they would protect someone with them. I'm glad I never had to find out if that was true.

But don't ever let what anybody else thinks keep you from being as smart as you can get. Knowledge is power. It can be used to get you far, but only if you use it for positive things. The world knows that the strong take from the weak, but the smart take from the strong.

Make Good Decisions:

Perhaps the greatest skill you can ever acquire, and the most important message we could ever communicate, is to learn to make good decisions.

Decision-making is both an instinctive and learned behavior. As human beings, we are hard-wired for decision-making: the fight or flight instinct is a basic human survival mechanism for making choices. In our modern world, the choices you must make go way beyond fight or flight when facing a wild animal, but they can be no less key to your survival.

Saying the wrong thing at the wrong time to the wrong person could result in anything from being grounded by parents to suspended by a teacher, being arrested by a police officer, to getting capped (shot).

Choosing to cut a class, shoplift a candy bar, or use a gun can have far-reaching impact that you didn't want.

So, make good decisions. Here's how:
- Consider the problem – What is the real problem and the root of it?

- What choices are there? - Consider all your options and the result of each.

- What do you want the end result to be? Consider your best goal.

- Choose the option that best helps you attain your goal (short & long-term goals).

Don't Take the Blame for the Other Guy

The code of silence in the streets makes some brothers take the weight for things that they didn't do. This is foolish. Each man has to take responsibility for the things that he does.

If you get blamed for something, and are about to be penalized for it, and you know who actually did it, then you should take that weight off of yourself. Do you think your friends would go to jail for you? Think hard about that one. In most desperate situations, it becomes every man for himself.

Just about every major religion states that you will be judged alone by the Almighty when you die. It's the same way on earth. You come into the world alone and you leave it alone. You are judged individually on a daily basis. Credit companies judge you. Insurance companies judge you. Realtors judge you. Teachers judge you. You are judged by coaches, employers, the police, and your peers.

Make sure that when you are judged it is for your own actions. There is nothing worse than getting a fine or jail time for something that you did not do. People say that the rapper Shine is doing time for Puff Daddy. I don't know what his involvement with the shootout in that New York club was, but he seems to be the only one doing time for it. If he let himself be bought by promises of fame or money, then he is truly a fool. You can't get back the time you spend in jail. Let's hope this rumor is false.

Let People Know You are Coming Over

It's not always a good idea to drop in on people unannounced. You never know if you are interrupting someone's thoughts, or interfering with some family matter.

As a young black man, you have to be extremely careful dropping in on people, especially at night. The presence of a strange young brother at someone's door at night is a cause of fear, not only for white people, but also for many older black people.

With all of the crime going on in our communities, some nervous homeowners answer their doors at night with a weapon. They see news accounts of home invasions on the news, and they don't like unannounced guests at night.

If the police grab you on your way to someone's house at night, and that person doesn't know you are coming, then you have no alibi. You can be blamed for something that you did not do. Look at the newspapers. Every week you see brothers released from prison because they were cleared on DNA evidence. Many were picked out of line-ups and didn't have an alibi about where they were going at the time of the crime.

If you are interested in a certain young lady, let her know if you plan on stopping by her house. You never know what you might find. Her parents might think that you are discourteous for coming without calling. You might not be the only brother trying to talk to her. You could be infringing on some family time or gathering. You could be getting in the way of her studying.

Even when people tell you to stop by anytime, you should still call in advance. You never know. They might not be home.

Political Survival

Never Consider Yourself a Minority

You are not a minority.

Why do black people continually call themselves minorities? We seek minority housing, minority education, minority financial development, minority this and minority that. We will call ourselves a minority anytime that it seems beneficial to us. Using this category to get a break for yourself is okay, but don't let yourself believe that we are a minority.

Are we really a minority? I don't think so. There may be less black people in America than white people, but when you look at the world, there are many more people of color. Look at all of the people of Africa. They are various shades of colors. Almost none of them would be considered white.

Go south of the border to Mexico and Central America. Are any of those people white? Most of the Afro, Hispanic, and indigenous people of South America aren't white either.

Go on over to Asia. There are a billion people in China alone. None of them are white. That's not even counting the folks in India, Pakistan, Iran, Iraq, and the rest of the Asian and Middle Eastern (Afro-Asiatic) countries.

When you look at the world, white people are actually a minority. Only when you limit your thinking to the United

States of America is when black people can be seen as minorities. Expand your thinking beyond the borders of this country, and you will see that you are part of the majority. You have brothers and sisters all over the world. How could you be a minority? There is nothing minor about you.

Save the Race Card for Important Issues

There was a group of girls who used to hang in the school hallways and end up late for every class. Once I saw them in the hall sitting on a radiator when I knew they were supposed to be in a math class. I asked them why they weren't in class. They told me that the teacher locked the door because they were five minutes late. Furthermore, they said that the teacher was a racist for not letting them in.

I laughed at the absurdity of their remark. They said, "What's so funny?" I asked them if the teacher had let any other students into the classroom. They said he let everyone in but the three of them. I said, "Aren't they black too?" They looked at me confused.

You see they played the race card when they really didn't have one. The race card should only be played in serious situations. Think of it as an ace, or a trump card. You don't just play your best cards without thinking first. If you waste an ace, you may lose the entire game.

When you accuse someone of being a racist, you need to have a good reason.

The girls in this situation are like a lot of people who cry racism when they aren't doing the right thing. I'm not saying that you won't have racist situations coming at you in

America. What I'm saying is pick your battles wisely. Remember, you can't blame all of your problems on the white man.

Remember the boy who kept crying wolf? After a while, no one believed him. Then one day the wolf paid a visit.

There is a difference between prejudice, bigotry and racism. If someone looks at you and thinks something negative about you because you're black, that means they are prejudiced. They pre-judged you. If someone wants to keep you from doing something because you're black, that's bigotry.

However, if someone uses the authority or power of their position to deny you opportunity or advancement because of your race, that's racism.

An old lady who clutches her purse tighter because a young black man is walking behind her is not being racist. That's prejudice. A teacher who says, "You kids from the projects can't learn" isn't being racist. That's bias. But when a company makes a practice of not giving black employees the same chance for promotions or raises that are given to white employees, that's racism. There's a difference.

The World Doesn't Revolve Around You

The world does not revolve around you or your wishes. The world will still move on whatever happens to you. Remember that and you will be able to keep the world and your life in perspective.

Every young rapper or ball player who appears on shows like MTV Cribs has a poster of the movie Scarface in his house. You would think that this was in honor of some real person instead of a movie character. Scarface's motto was "The world is yours." He thought that he could have the world revolve around him. As a matter of fact, he had a spinning globe of the earth, with that very motto, hanging like a chandelier in his mansion.

That idea that he could be the center of the universe is a part of what led to his very violent death. He lived with no humility, and it led to a predictable end.

You are going to learn in life that most of the time no one cares about your problems but you and your family. If you die tomorrow, the cost of milk will still be the same.

We are all like individual planets. We all have to follow the laws of the universe, or we will surely collide and crumble. Moons revolve around planets. Planets revolve around suns. Suns revolve around galaxies, and we are just tiny specks of dust in comparison. Think of that whenever your head gets too big.

In their song, "Respect Yourself," the Staples Singers say, "If you walk about thinking that the world owes you something 'cause you're here, you're going out the world backwards like you did when you first came here."

Let the Cops Do Their Jobs

You should never dime on a brother if you can help it, but sometimes it needs to be done. It is no secret that most crimes committed against young brothers are committed by other young brothers. This is truly disturbing.

If a brother commits a crime against you, don't take the law into your own hands. You could end up being victimized twice – once by the victim and once by the law.

Your best bet would be to call the cops and let them do their jobs. If you know who broke into your house or robbed someone in your family or hurt one of your neighbors, call the police. Don't go outside with a gun looking for vengeance. You will probably end up locked up or shot.

Revenge never works. It only starts a cycle of back and forth violence. Call the cops. They get paid to solve crimes – not you.

If someone in your community is harmed by crime, and you witness it, you need to step up and dial 9-1-1. Leave an anonymous tip if you prefer, but don't let the crooks take over your 'hood.

The World Isn't Fair

If you are looking for the world to be fair, then you have another thought coming. Fair is a place you go to eat cotton candy. Fair is a light color. Fair is a place of fantasy. As far as fair being a balanced situation is concerned, there is no fair.

The playing field is unbalanced against young black men. You will always be judged by a different set of rules. You will always be playing uphill, against a stronger opponent. The referees are always going to give you more penalties than the other team. Your end of the stick will always be a little shorter. You will always be outnumbered and outgunned. Despite all of that, you can still succeed. Countless brothers have made it in spite of the odds against them. Why can't you?

You know the world isn't fair for you, so get over it! You know you will have to work harder, so do it. You know you have to dig deeper, so get to it. Sure, you start farther back than the regular starting line, but that doesn't mean you can't catch up. You just have to run faster and jump higher.

Diamonds are created by the pressure put on carbon from centuries of weight pressing on it. Life isn't fair and it puts extra pressure on you. Become a diamond. (Be the bling.)

Stand

Sooner or later, there will come a time in your life when you will have to stand and give your voice to a cause. There are so many issues affecting young black people that there is a cause for everyone.

There are employment issues. There are education issues. There are housing issues. There are issues of destructive advertising on billboards in our neighborhoods. There are issues of unjust wars, unfair taxes, negative portrayals in the media, lack of city services, and an unequal court system.

All of these situations can use one more brother fighting for them. If we don't stand up, we can't possibly expect any change. Remember, it is the squeaky wheel that gets the oil.

Someone much wiser than us once said, "If you don't stand for something, you will fall for everything." Look around you. The family needs you. The community needs you. The nation needs you. And, the world needs you to stand up, put your shoulder to the wheel, and help us push.

Love the Planet

We can't worry about the city, state or federal government messing up the world if we are doing it too. Every bit of trash on the streets of black neighborhoods was put there by black people. Every window that was broken, every broken 40-ounce malt liquor bottle, and every bit of graffiti was put there by our people. We have to start thinking differently.

Maybe we can't attend rallies about endangered whales, but there are rallies for endangered young black men. They could use your support.

If you are into wearing a lot of diamonds, remember that they probably came from some mine in South Africa where miners don't get proper pay. We need to realize that a lot of our habits affect the world.

When we pollute our environment, we cannot expect to be living healthy. If our environment is dirty, how can we be clean? If we bathe in dirty water, will we be cleansed?

Recycle those cans and bottles. Teach the little kids to put their candy wrappers in the trash. Make sure your car is tuned up and not spewing toxic waste. Put liners in your trashcans and put lids on them. Make sure that you don't leave trashcans out all week. Grow some plants or trees – they help clean the air.

Live Life Like a Commando Mission

I loved to read comic books when I was young. One of my favorites was Sergeant Fury and the Howling Commandoes. What was so cool about the commandoes was that they were a diverse group of big, strong guys who could each do something unique, but could also do some of everything. They could operate every type of machine or system, speak several languages, dress in any types of style and, most importantly, they could survive in any type of condition or hardship. They were given a mission and they used every means imaginable to accomplish it, and they never gave up until they did.

You don't have to be in the army to adopt that kind of thinking and use if for your life.

As you live your life, young brother, always be on a mission. Learn how to operate machines and vehicles safely and responsibly. Be able to think quickly and clearly. Learn to adapt to any situation, always be aware and alert. And never give up until the job is done.

Sexual Survival

Don't Fight Over Girls

In January of '05, an 18 year old was killed in front of Dobbins High School in Philadelphia. The young brother was not a student of the school. In fact, he had dropped out of another high school in Philly earlier that year.

His assailant didn't go to Dobbins High School either. He shot the boy on the front walk of the school and neither of them had anything to do with the school.

Later it was found that their connection to the school was a 16-year-old girl. One brother dead, another going to jail for life over a girl. They let their emotions destroy them.

As a young man, you will surely experience heartbreak. Give it some time. Deal with it. Then move on. There are many more girls to meet. There are girls outside of your small circle or neighborhood. Don't be lazy. Go meet some. There are many fish in the sea.

If you love yourself, you would never hurt someone else over a girl. If you thought you had love and lost love, then welcome to the human race. There have been millions of songs written about it. On the other hand, there are millions of songs about finding new love.

Look Around Before You Dance

You never know if that girl that you really want to dance with has a boyfriend. Take the time before you dance to do a quick survey of the room. Look towards the entrance when people arrive. Did she come solo, with a group of girlfriends, or with a mixed group of male and female friends? If she walks into the party with one guy, then you had better be careful with your approach.

Most fights at parties and dances are over jealousy. Many young brothers feel slighted if their girlfriend dances with someone else. Even if it is a fast dance, where the partners don't actually touch each other, some guys still get jealous.

What you see as a bit of innocent socializing could be the beginning of the end of the party. Not all brothers are secure in themselves so, therefore, they can't be secure in their relationships. These are the brothers that you need to steer clear of. Blind envy makes them feel that you are trying to steal their woman.

So, make sure that the girl that you want to dance with is unattached, or you could be in for trouble.

Use the Right Head

Sex is something that we all want. Young men reach puberty and the first thing we think of is girls. Hormones start acting up and we start doing all sorts of dumb things to attract the opposite sex. Nothing is wrong with that. The problem comes in when we don't think before we act. That is called thinking with the wrong head.

When you think with the wrong head, you usually do the wrong thing. Thinking with your smaller head will get you into trouble.

Your small head does not have a brain. All it has is feeling. All it can feel is pleasure or pain. It can't get you out of problems; it can only get you into them.

Looking for instant pleasure is acting on impulse. We don't need to be impulsive. A minute's worth of pleasure could cause a lifetime of pain. Just because your body tells you that you want sex is no reason to do it without thinking first. Do you have a condom? What will you do if you get this girl pregnant? What will you do if you get an S.T.D.? If you can't answer these questions, then you are thinking with the wrong head.

Don't Bash Gay Brothers

What other people do with their sex lives is nobody else's business. There is no need worrying about what the other guy does. If you are gay or straight it doesn't matter. You are still a black man in America.

Everyone has their own interest in life. Everyone has their own life to live. We can't judge other people because we are not perfect.

Would you refuse to have your life saved by a gay doctor? Would you refuse knowledge from a gay teacher? Would you refuse service from a gay person to fix your heater, air conditioner, refrigerator, or car? If you think so, think again. You've probably already had that happen and been unaware of it.

Let brothers who don't think like you live the way they want to live. If you are heterosexual, then you should take the positive view that there will be more girls left for you. If you are gay, you have the right not to be picked on. Gay brothers are still our brothers.

Beware the Down Low

Every time you turn on African American discussion shows on T.V. or the radio these days, the topic that comes up very often is men on the "down low."

These are black men who have wives or girlfriends and still have sex with other men. I know it sounds strange, but these men don't consider themselves either bisexual or homosexual.

Now don't get me wrong. I'm not judging anybody's sexual preference. If you are gay, that is your business. The problem is one of honesty. If you lie to your wife or girlfriend, you will lie to anyone. How can you trust a brother who is living a lie?

This guy puts his female partner in jeopardy every time he has sex with her. He could bring home any number of deadly diseases to a woman who could be completely unaware.

Your best bet is to stay away from brothers who are on the down low. Honesty is always the best policy. You don't want to be surprised by an awkward situation or invitation. If you are in a situation where you thought the brothers were straight, but you find out otherwise, just quickly and quietly leave. Don't make a scene – just split.

Financial Survival

Never Let Friends Use Your Name

If you have a friend who is having trouble getting something in his name, don't let him use yours. Don't put your name on a car, phone, or credit card for someone else. I don't care how well you know them, you are asking for trouble.

You should know right away that something is wrong if they can't get these things in their own names. The next question is why can't they get one of their family members to sign for them? The answer is that their family members probably already told them no. You see, they know this person better than you.

All you have to do is turn on the television and tune into any one of the court T.V. shows. On any given day, someone is suing someone else over an unpaid phone bill, an overused credit card, or a car accident that they didn't have anything to do with. Their only connection to the problem was that their name was involved.

If your friend has had bad credit before, he will probably have bad credit again. Just because his own name is not on the card is no guarantee that he is going to change his ways. If he continues, he will destroy your credit along with his.

If your friend can't buy a car because he doesn't have a license or insurance, don't let him use yours to get a car.

There is a reason why he doesn't have a license or insurance. It probably has something to do with the fact that they get a lot of tickets. If the car is in your name, then his tickets become your tickets. You will probably lose your license too.

The same goes for credit cards, home mortgages, bank loans, and anything else involving money. If their credit is no good, why would you let them use your name? They have already proven that they don't pay their bills and have problems paying their bills. Why are they going to change their ways now? Don't put yourself in a situation where a so-called friend can destroy your credit.

It's important to understand that, in America, credit and the way banks look at you are key to getting houses, cards, and the things you will want. Getting credit from a bank or credit card company is how it works in America, and you have to protect yourself from things that will mess up your credit like not paying your bills on time, overspending, identity theft and letting other people use your name.

When your friends ask to borrow your name, tell them you can't afford it.

Make Out a Will

Black men statistically have the shortest life expectancies of any other racial group in America. It's a fact, not a prediction. One of the many problems with that is that too many black men die without a will.

When you die without a will, there is no way for anyone to know what your last wishes are. Who gets your house? Who gets your car? Who gets control of your bank accounts and other assets?

You want to be in control of the things that you have worked hard for. You want them to go to people who deserve them or people who will take good care of them. You don't want your things going to someone who didn't like you while you were alive.

If you have assets that other family members don't know about, then you really need a will. If family members don't know about your private bank accounts, insurance policies, stocks, safe deposit boxes, etc., the government could get their hands on them after a certain amount of time. Your family could automatically forfeit any claims to your assets if they sit idle over time.

There is also a thing called a living will. This determines what will happen if you can no longer live on your own. Don't leave it up to family members to decide if you should live on life support machinery or not.

If you are in a situation where you can no longer move or are in a coma and considered brain dead, do you want to keep living like that or have someone pull the plug? Some people feel that they want to cling to life to the end. Some feel that miracles happen everyday. Others can't stand the thought of not being able to move. This is a very difficult decision for family members to have to make at a time of pain.

Whichever way you decide is your own business. You should, however, be the one who makes that decision. All of these problems can be avoided if you have a will.

Stay Away From Pay Day Loans

Predatory lenders prey on African Americans. They set up loan offices in neighborhoods of color because they know that so many black people are hurting financially. You can get a loan from these companies, but it is rarely worth it. These companies are like legal loan sharks.

They charge so much in interest that many folks have difficulty paying their loans back on time. When you pay late, there is a penalty involved. The longer you take to pay, the higher the penalty fee. Sometimes you will end up paying more in fees than the actual loan.

Don't dig yourself into that financial hole. Think twice before borrowing money to pay your bills. Your best bet is to not make any outstanding bills for yourself. Then you won't need to borrow from these loan sharks. Remember, if you owe a bill and you borrow money to pay that bill, you still owe that same money plus interest to your lender. You will be running around in circles like a dog with his tail cut off.

If you have an emergency need for money, try to borrow it from an established bank. The last resort is to borrow from family, but even this beats a very high interest loan.

If you do the math, you will find that these loans are a very bad idea for anybody. The problem for us is that these companies target desperate communities, and we are a desperate community. They advertise on radio stations that we listen to. You see them on daytime T.V., when unemployed people are home, and most of their offices are convenient to public transportation. These companies will cause you to lose your car, lose your house, and lose your bank account. They can even take you to court and garnish your paycheck. Guess who has to pay the court cost. In most states, it's you.

If there is something that you don't need, do without it. If there is something that you need and don't have enough money, put it on layaway. You can pay a little at a time without needing a loan.

Pay Attention to Detail or Get Fired

A recent story on ABC News stated that more than 50% of all black men in New York City are unemployed. There were various reasons given for the problem. One reason given was that no one wants to hire them because of the color of their skin. Another was that white employers would rather hire black women, especially in high visibility situations. The one reason that they did seem to stress was education. Of the three brothers who were profiled for the story, two of them had dropped out of high school. The third brother had no skill or trade.

If we want to become employable, we have to pay attention to detail. We have to get certified in trades and unions. We have to go through all the necessary steps to get internships and take classes in the things that will make us employable.

Nobody owes us anything, especially if we don't pay attention to details.

Many young brothers who get jobs can't keep them because they don't follow orders well. Many feel as if they are being chumped by the white man when they are following orders. This keeps us from paying close attention when we are given orders. We often sabotage ourselves before we even get started. We give people ample reasons to fire us. We play right into that game.

If you need specific tools for a job and you don't have them with you for the job, you will probably be fired.

If you are supposed to wear a certain type of uniform, and you don't, you will probably be fired.

If you go to work in clothes that are wrinkled or dirty, you will probably be fired.

If your clothes smell like smoke or alcohol, you will probably be fired.

If you smell funky, you will probably be fired.

If you go to work late, you will probably be fired.

If you like to argue with your boss, you will probably be fired.

If your paperwork doesn't cover your ass (C.Y.A.), you will probably be fired.

If your supplies or products come up short, you will probably be fired.

If you are caught doing drugs or drinking on the job, you will probably be fired.

Financial Survival

With all of the bad stuff happening in the world, these seem like small things. They aren't small things to the people who own the companies. Those people got into their positions by paying attention to detail.

Keep Your Receipts

You should have a box or a drawer where you keep all of your receipts. Anytime that you buy something, you should keep your paperwork in it. There are good reasons for doing this.

You never know if you will have to return something to the place where it was purchased. Most stores will not give a refund or exchange unless you can prove you bought it there. How do you prove you bought it? The receipt!

If there is ever a dispute over ownership of any of your belongings, you can end all arguments with a receipt. Proof of purchase can shut the mouths of anyone who is trying to claim your property.

Saving your receipts while you are still young will get you into the practice for later when you have to worry about income taxes. Your receipts could mean the difference between you getting a tax refund or paying a tax fine.

Your receipts let you know when you bought something in case the product needs to be serviced. Some products are recalled because of problems or defects. Without a receipt, you won't be able to be compensated.

Small Problems Versus Big Problems

A small problem is easy to handle. Large problems take much more time and money to handle. Most large problems start out small. A flood was once a leak. A gash was once a cut, and an avalanche was once a snowball. Handle your problems while they are still small.

When my son was new to driving, he got a bunch of parking tickets. It was bad enough that he disregarded the parking signs near the community college that he was attending, but he made the situation much worse.

He had seven parking tickets that were worth about $25 each. That's more than $175 worth of tickets if they were paid within 15 days of the original citations. He hid the tickets from me and his mother. After the 15-day grace period, the tickets were now worth $40 apiece. That's over $280 worth of tickets. Well, it would have been if he hadn't put it off again.

About a month later, his car was booted by the city, then impounded. To get his car back, he had to pay an impound fee of $75, a towing fee of $65, the $280 for the tickets, and another $50 in fees and cost. The final cost was close to $500 just to get his car back. What a waste of money. All of this could have been solved for a lot cheaper if he had taken care of the problem in a timely manner.

I don't care what the situation is – an argument, a car problem, home repair, school problems, matters of the heart, or whatever – try to solve it before it escalates into something that you can't handle. Attack problems when they happen. Solving a small problem will keep it from becoming a big problem.

Don't Put People Down Who Have Less

One of the worst things you can do is put down people who have less than you. If you have one hundred dollar Timberlands and one of your friends or classmates is wearing $30 boots from K-Mart, that does not give you the right to feel superior. Especially if you did not earn the money to buy the boots yourself.

Just because your parents will spend money on things that are unnecessary, that doesn't give you any real advantage in life. All it does is waste money. The person with $30 boots parents may be paying a $200,000 mortgage and saving for college tuition. A young brother once told me that Timberlands are better because you can stand in six inches of water for an hour without ever getting your feet wet. I asked him when was the last time he stood in six inches of water for an hour. He had no answer, and started to become angry at me. He said that I was a cheap old man who didn't know anything about fashion. I told him that those boots were made for work, not fashion. I could have come down harder on him if I wanted to. After all, he was wearing work boots and didn't even have a job.

Advertisers count on black people to be wasteful with our money. They know that many of us spend unwisely. That's why we will buy mountain bikes in a town where there are no hills. We will buy diver's watches that are waterproof up to

100 feet deep, and never even swim in it. We buy $150 basketball shoes and never even touch a ball. Some of us buy fast cars and have no place to go. I've seen young people driving a Lexus to drop off their child and girlfriend at the homeless shelter. It can get to be ridiculous, but we will spend just to say we have something better than someone else. Then we talk about those who don't have as much as us. We can be our own worst enemy.

Leave people alone. The person with less material things might have more talent than you. They could have more spirituality, drive, determination, wisdom, understanding, awareness, courage, resourcefulness, or just more common sense.

Being materialistic (caught up in wanting material things and stuff) is part of the brainwash, money-grab that gets people in debt and makes the rich get richer while you stay broke.

Learn a Trade

You always hear old folks talking about having something to fall back on. By this, they mean having an extra skill that you can use when money gets tight.

Too many young brothers feel that they are going to work one job and that they will be covered for life. Well, people get fired. People get laid off. Businesses close down or move out of town. What are you going to do if you find yourself in that type of situation?

The best thing that you can do to prepare yourself and be ready for any layoff is to have more than one skill. Just because you are a store clerk doesn't mean you can't also be a carpenter. Just because you wear a suit and tie to work doesn't mean you can't also be a plumber. Just because you have been a company worker doesn't mean you can't work on your own as a landscaper, mason, electrician, appliance repair person, computer technician, carpet layer, musician, driver, writer, photographer, cook, or any other skilled job. All you have to do is be willing to learn something new.

By the same token, if you are a person who already works with his hands, then you need to also know a job you can work with your mind. You never know when your skills as a barber or a bricklayer will start to diminish. If you have something to fall back on, you will always be in demand.

Everything you learn to do will come into play at some point in your life. When you own your house, you will likely have to be the carpenter, plumber, electrician, painter, mover, accountant, manager, executive and everything else. Learn a trade for your future use in work and home.

Don't Live from Case to Case

Some people sue so often that they live their lives from case to case. When you are done harm by some person or company, then you should sue. The problem for everyone comes in when people sue over and over again, or when they sue for something frivolous.

There are people who fake all kinds of accidents just to get their hands on some insurance. They have false slip and falls, staged auto accidents, phony escalator slips, pseudo-stress, and a bunch of other made up injuries and medical conditions in order to "get paid."

Well, let's call it what it really is. It is theft. In order to get paid, you have to work. This is not working. This is swindling money. So, don't call it getting paid. If you want to get paid, then you need to get a job. Many states are cracking down hard on insurance fraud and false claims. You might end up with the kind of case that lands you in the joint.

People who live from case to case usually owe out much of their money before they ever get a check. Insurance companies usually hold out until the very end before they pay any actual money. It could be three or four years before they put a check in your hand.

What will you do for money while you wait? You can't be seen doing any heavy work or driving if you are hurt. So, you will probably do a lot of borrowing based on the fact that you have a check on the way. When you get that check, you have to pay back the money you borrowed.

Mental Survival

Stay Flexible

Don't be so rigid in your ways that you can't change. Sometimes plans and ideas don't work out the way that you dream they would. That doesn't mean you can't be just as successful in some other area of life.

Many young brothers unrealistically think that they are going to become professional athletes. The idea of playing in the NFL, the NBA or major league baseball is something that most boys want to do. Sure it is possible for it to happen, but it is highly improbable, especially if you are not already an all-star.

The NBA recruits about sixty new players out of all who are drafted each year. That's sixty out of the thousands of outstanding college players across the country. That's not even counting the guys coming directly out of high school and the guys from Europe, Africa and China.

Young brothers need to be able to stay flexible, to have a plan B and a plan C. So what you are not going to the pros. Most of your friends aren't either.

So what you didn't get the job you wanted. Keep looking until you find one. You didn't get into the college that you wanted? Find one that wants you. Can't afford a car? Ride the bus. You can still attain many of your dreams and reach your goals if you remain flexible.

Know Why You Do What You Do

There should be a reason for just about anything that you do in public. You should always be able to explain why you did something. If your answer to why you do anything is "I don't know," people will definitely think you are crazy. Just saying "because..." is not an explanation for doing something.

Animals act on instinct. They know why they do everything that they do. They hunt to eat, they sleep for rest, they have sex to cure their need to mate, etc. Human beings, on the other hand, do many things that they can't explain. Sometimes this can get you into trouble. When parents, teachers, coaches, or cops ask why you did something, you need to have a concrete answer. It could be the difference between passing and failing, punishment and reward, opportunity or setback.

Take the time to think. Some things only require a second to think about. Some things need more time. Sometimes you should sleep on it before you decide to do something. Exercise your brain by using it. Think, and know why you do what you do.

Everything you do has consequences. Some of them have positive results, and some are disastrous. If you know why you do something, then you can understand the purpose of your actions. If the purpose is unnecessary or negative, then don't do it.

Big Thoughts, Small Pleasures

Think big thoughts, enjoy small pleasures.

It's good to want all of the good things that life has to offer. We all want a nice house, an expensive ride, and lots of hip clothes to wear. We all want that high-paying job for doing something that we actually like doing. We all want to be accepted into the coolest clubs, and be recognized by celebrities. Hey, some of us even want to be President of the United States, and that's okay.

Remember, when you are working towards those big things, don't lose sight of small things that make life worthwhile.

Stop and smell the roses that you have been passing by everyday. Sit and listen to different parts of songs, besides the drums and words. Eat something that you like and take the time to chew and savor like it is your last meal. Walk in the sunshine and feel the warmth of God. Do a favor for an old person and see the look of relief on their faces. Climb a tree and relax. Have a glass of lemonade during the summer. Go swimming, ride a bike, or play some ball. See how good you feel afterwards.

Look at a baby. He doesn't need much to make him happy. All he needs is food and someone to change his diapers and give him love.

Count your blessings if you have good, shelter and clothing. Count them and shout for joy!

You Da Man!

Don't ever listen to anyone who tells you that young black men don't count. The world has been copying your styles for a long time. Go anywhere in the world and you will see young folk involved in hip-hop clothing styles and rapping in their various languages.

This is not a new phenomenon. Europeans welcomed black jazz musicians to their countries after WWI. Ragtime piano, the blues, bebop, soul, rhythm and blues, funk and just about every other form of black music are received all over the world.

How could you be a nobody when everybody wants to look like you? No matter how foolishly you dress, the rest of the world still wants to be like you. I have to crack up when I see young guys in other countries with their hats on backwards and their pants sagging while wearing an NFL or NBA jersey.

You are the man, so stand up and be counted. In case you haven't noticed, the world is watching you. This brings you a responsibility. Don't let the world think that you are a mindless, violent, non-working, wife-beating, drug-dealing, bank-robbing, shoplifting, alcoholic, neighborhood-destroying, gangster fool.

You set the standard. You da man!

Make Your Music

The group, Earth, Wind and Fire, said it best back in the '70s. "If you sing a song today, you will make a better way." And we believe it. Just about any situation will seem better if you can manage to sing.

Go back to slavery. Without those field chants, many of the slaves would not have had a chance to holler out their pain. Without the blues, many a sharecropper would not have been able to articulate the pain of post-slavery. We can even see it in rap. The shouts from the street are broken into rhymes and put into verses that allow the pain to escape from the mouths of rappers.

Find a song that helps you when you feel down. Find another song for when you need inspiration. Find a song that will make you want to uplift the race. Find a song that you can sing to kids. Find a song that you can sing with family or friends. Then sing it!

Rhythm nation, create things of beauty. Learn to play an instrument. Music is a healing force of the universe. Melody and harmony are in the world all around us. The lilting tune of birds whistling back and forth. The bass, baritone blend of a Cadillac or Buick car horn. Being in tune and in harmony are concepts of life which are put into play and can be perfected through music.

The first instruments were the voice and the hands. So, sing rap, orate, doo-wop in the church choir, glee club, boys choir, stairwell, schoolyard, or on the corner. Harmonize, call and respond.

Clap, play sticks, tambourine, congas, bongos, traps, djembe, Bata. Learn the ancient rhythms which brought forth jazz, blues, gospel, R&B, soul, rock and roll, disco, hip-hop, funk, fusion and more.

Don't just listen. Make some music yourself.

Beware the Black Monolith

Television producers and marketers seem to think that all African Americans are monolithic. They think that all black people like the same shows, wear the same clothes, smoke the same cigarettes, and that somehow we all know each other. You might think that's funny, but check deeper.

When the Nielsen television ratings came out a couple of years ago, they said that "The Parkers" was the number one show watched by African Americans. I'm African American and I have never watched that particular show before. Perhaps it came on while I was watching something else that I liked more. Maybe the previews didn't look that entertaining to me. Whatever the reason, I didn't watch the show that African Americans were supposed to watch. Does that make me any less black?

The media can distort images of African Americans very easily by lumping us all into very neat categories. They would have you believe that most of the people on welfare are black women. Tell the truth. When you think of a person on welfare, you think of a black woman with kids, don't you?

If you look at television, you would hear the words "black youth" and immediately think crime. This is a shame because most young black men are not committing crimes. The problem is that a video about a sensible brother doing the right thing won't sell. So, the record companies keep churning out videos about sex and violence. The rest of the world sees this and they assume that all black people must act this way.

You Represent Your Family

If you could hear the language of young black people in Philadelphia public schools, you would be ashamed. Sure, we cussed when we were growing up, but not in front of adults. And the girls certainly didn't call each other bitches, unless they were in an argument or fight.

Bill Cosby was one of those adults who happened to hear how our kids carry on. He spoke about it publicly. Whether you agree with The Cos or not, you must admit that it looks bad. It looks bad for you and your family. It makes people wonder how you were raised. If your parents are good, hard working people who did their best to raise you, don't go dragging their name in the dirt.

Imagine your family having to tell people that you are in jail instead of in school. What if all of your family has to sit through a newscast about some crime that you committed?

Everything that you do reflects on your family. If you throw trash in the street or on the floors at school, then you will be seen as trash. It does not matter how well you are dressed, people will still see you as trash.

If you spit on floors indoors, act rowdy to be noticed, bully others, cuss in front of respected elders, and refuse to act civil, you make your whole family look bad. Unfortunately, people judge many by the acts of a few. If you don't think this is true, check out how many times one of your teachers has to say, "Do you do that in front of your mother?".

Light Skin – Dark Skin

Many African Americans get caught up in the light-skinned, dark-skinned game. This is really a trip because people who are trying to rise need to help each other.

This goes back to the days of slavery when the lighter-skinned slaves usually worked in the big house, while the darker-skinned slaves worked in the fields. This caused a lot of resentment among the field slaves, and that is exactly what the slave owners wanted. People who are divided will never win.

There was the false notion put out by the slave masters that the lighter you are the more breaks you got. Sure, some of the lighter-skinned slaves ate better, but when you get right down to it, they were still slaves. They had no freedom and they were usually the children of slaves who were raped by brutal owners.

The brainwashing was so complete that many historically black colleges and universities used to make you send a picture along with your application. These black schools seemed to be worried about balancing the amounts of light and dark-skinned students that they accepted. They figured that they needed a certain amount of light-skinned blacks to graduate from their schools because they would be more easily accepted in American businesses.

Mental Survival

Who knows? Maybe there is some truth to what the old folks used to say: "If you're white, you're right. If you're brown, stick around. If you're black, get back." If other people treat us that way, it doesn't mean you need to act like that towards each other.

If you ever make a trip to Africa, you will see that there are black people of all colors. The people of Morocco and Libya are very light-skinned. The people of the Sudan and the Congo are very dark. The Ethiopians run from light to dark. The one thing that they have in common is that they are all Africans. As a light-skinned brother with locks, a well-traveled, Middle Eastern man once told me that if I walked down the street in Lagos, Nigeria, no one would think I was not Nigerian, until I spoke.

African Americans run the gamut from light, bright and damn near white, to deep dark mahogany. Don't assume that you have an advantage because you are light or dark. You are still a black person in America.

Be a Myth Buster

Some folks subscribe to the myth that all young black kids are troublemakers. Don't give them reasons to keep thinking this. Some people expect you to drop out of school based on where you live and what your grades were in elementary school.

These people ignore the fact that there are more success stories than failure stories in the black communities. More black kids graduate than drop out. You wouldn't know it by watching T.V.

There are so many myths about young black men, and they are told so often, that the average person has a hard time not believing them.

Don't feed into the myths that young black men are violent, disrespectful, non-family oriented, abandoners of our children, wife beating, criminal minded, immoral, ignorant, non-political, illiterate deviants of society. Believe it or not, many people of all races see young black folks this way. Don't give them any reasons to keep believing it.

The negative stereotypes, myths, and outright lies about black men have a long and sordid history. Black soldiers in World War II had to endure the ridiculous notion that people in Europe thought they had tails.

Mental Survival

For many years in this country, some folk regarded it as fact that black people were lazy, shiftless and stupid (overlooking the fact that we had labored for hundreds of years from 'can't see in the morning to can't see at night' without a single paycheck). So long-standing and pervasive were many of the lies that entire institutions and scientific theories developed which gave credence to the untrue and often unbelievable lies.

In your everyday life, as you go about doing what you have to do to make your life better or to enjoy yourself, show the world that none of the lies put on black men are true in your case.

Show that you are intelligent, motivated and energetic. Show that you care for yourself, other people, and the world. Let the world see that you are strong physically, mentally, and emotionally; that you are the descendant of the strongest people ever on the planet. The people who survived the holocaust of slavery and racism to become world leaders in every field of industry, science and academia.

You are the son of kings and queens. Let that be the only myth that can be applied to you.

Use Your Ju-Ju

Africans call It Ju-Ju. Natives call it medicine. In the Caribbean and down south, it might be called voodoo. In the 'hood, it's mojo.

Whatever it's called, black folks are in tune with the vibration and rhythm of the universe and people. So, use your psychic, ESP, mental telepathy, intuition, to read and understand people and situations to work for you and to avoid trouble.

If it feels good, do it. If it don't fit, don't force it. Your Ju-Ju will let you know what decisions to make. It warns you with signs. It puts that tingle in your gut. It flashes signs of danger in your mind. It is so real that it is a part of your being. Use it.

If something doesn't feel right, it probably isn't right. If the party feels tense, go to another one. If you think someone is going to cause a scuffle, move on. You know when these things are going to happen. You can sense a negative vibe because of your Ju-Ju. When you got your mojo working, you will be a winner.

Survival of the Fittest

Man-Up

No one owes you anything. Face that fact. Deal with it and man-up!

The teacher didn't give you the grade that you thought you deserved. Don't sit around cussing. Figure out what you are doing wrong and do better.

Take responsibility for all that you do in school, work, home and in other situations. Be a man by doing the right things that you need to survive. Don't be one of those nuts who talk a good game but can't take care of himself and his family.

Speak up when you see injustice. Give well thought out opinions when asked. If there is a subject that you don't know anything about, be a man and admit that you don't.

If someone is trying to sell you something that you don't want, be man enough to tell them that you are not interested. If someone tries to get you to go somewhere you don't want to go, be man enough to tell them no.

There are going to be many times where you are going to be called upon to man up. If you live by the doctrine of doing the right thing and treating people the way you want to be treated, you will always be regarded as a true man.

Never Show Your Hand Too Soon

This is a gambler's phrase that can be applied to many facets of life. Here are some ways that it may apply to you.

I have a friend who bragged about the bargain that he got on a pair or really cool shoes. He told everyone about where they could get the shoes and the sizes that were available.

About two weeks later, everyone was getting ready for the spring dance. He knew that he was going to have on the sharpest shoes in the place. When he got to the party, he noticed that there were at least five other guys with the same shoes that he was wearing. One guy was wearing the exact same, two-toned color that he had. Now he was no longer unique. He was really just one person in the crowd.

What he should have done was waited until he got to the dance to tell about his shoes. He showed his cards too soon. It's called peeping your hole card.

Another friend, who was a songwriter, played his cards too soon also. He was so happy that a certain producer wanted to see his work, so he gave him a tape of his best songs.

About a year later, he heard the words to two of his songs on the radio. When he asked the producer for his share of the money, the producer acted like he didn't even know my friend. My friend sued in court and lost.

What he should have done was gotten a copyright on his work. He showed his hand too soon.

Try to avoid letting people know things too soon. Let them know only what they need to know. They will figure out the rest.

If You are Doing Wrong, Expect Punishment

Most guys who get locked up for something say that they saw it coming. The guys who trip me out are the ones who are surprised that they were arrested. I've talked with young brothers doing 20 years or more for killing another brother. They told me that even though they were carrying a gun, they didn't plan to shoot anybody.

It's weird. Drug dealers are surprised when they get busted for selling to an undercover cop. Thieves are surprised when they get caught with the goods. Carjackers are surprised when they crash the car. Druggies are surprised when they overdose. Red light runners are surprised when they get a ticket. People who have sex without protection are surprised when they get HIV. People who pull guns are surprised when they get shot.

I don't know where all of this shock and surprise comes from. I think too many young brothers feel invincible. We feel that bad things won't happen to us. But if you don't use your brain, you would easily find yourself in a bad situation. Bad situations for brothers usually lead to some sort of punishment.

So, stay positive, always do the right thing, and you won't have to get a surprise punishment.

It's What's Up Front that Counts

Satchel Page, one of the greatest pitchers of all time, did not get to pitch in the major leagues until the last part of his career. He spent most of his best years pitching in the old Negro Leagues, the Caribbean, and Central America. Some reporter once asked him if he regrets not being given a chance to pitch younger because he was black. Page replied, "I don't look back. Something might be gaining on me."

What he was basically saying was that it's what's up front that counts. You can't spend time holding onto grudges and beefs from the past. You have to look to the future.

No one is telling you to forgive and forget everything bad that has happened to you. Hopefully you learned a lesson from things that didn't go your way.

If you lose a game of sports, remember it's just a game. It has no bearing on your life. If you get dumped by someone you love, remember there are billions of other people on this planet. If you fail a test, study harder for the next one. If someone gives you the finger while you are driving, keep your eyes on the road. Remember, it's what's up front that counts.

The past can't be changed. The future? Who knows? As Satchel Page also said, "Maybe I'll pitch forever."

Winners Do What Losers Don't Want To

Magic Johnson, Mike Jordan and Larry Bird all have multiple championship rings. They each led their teams onto glorious victories and will all be in the Hall of Fame. They also share a common trait that made them the best. That thing that separated those great players from the good and average players is that they were willing to do more.

They say white men can't jump, but Larry Bird didn't have to. His accurate shooting gave him an edge. It didn't come naturally, he worked on it. Magic Johnson was always the first and last player at practice. He worked on his game, even after he was a champion.

Jordan didn't make the varsity on his first try, but he worked on his game. He worked on his strength. He did the things that the guys on the losing teams refused to do.

Look at a team that can't win in the playoffs. Those extra games wear down the teams that aren't in top physical shape. Guys who don't practice. Guys who disrupt instead of work are often popular, but they rarely ever win. Those who worked on the games and strength training had the physical advantage.

It goes beyond sports and into every phase of life. The best goods come from cooks who pay attention to detail. They

Survival of the Fittest

know how to select fresh fish, chicken and meats. They know the right amounts of seasonings. They keep up with new trends in goods by doing some extra reading. They keep the customers' taste buds happy and get paid well for their extra effort.

The lawyer whose team does the best research usually wins, regardless of how much money either started out with. The mechanic who continually studies can fix any car. He is the most valuable mechanic. He will probably make the most money. All of these winners are willing to do things that losers don't want to.

Just Go to the Rack

Moses Malone was one of the greatest basketball players of all time. The Philadelphia 76ers traded for Moses in 1983. They won the title that year, largely from the efforts of Mr. Malone. His rebounding ability was tremendous. He would jump two or three times to the other center's one jump.

Once during an after game interview, Moses was asked if there was a secret to his rebounding ability. Moses said that there was no secret, "I just go to the rack." By that he meant that he just tries very hard to outwork the other guys on the court. His determination not to be outworked was the key to his success. He just gritted his teeth and decided that he was going to hustle for every loose ball and guard the boards tenaciously.

We need to think about Moses Malone's words and apply them to everyday life. Go to the rack on your job. Go to the rack in school. Go to the rack for charities. Go to the rack for your family. Go to the rack to uplift the world.

When you feel like not doing your homework, suck it up and go to the rack. When you feel like not going to work, dig down deep and go to the rack. When you feel the pressure to give up or drop out, try one more time to go to the rack. That one rebound may just win the game.

Get Out of Harm's Way

If people around you are reckless, get away from them. Stay away from people, places and things that will cause you harm.

If you put yourself in harm's way, sooner or later you will be harmed. If everybody around you gets into trouble, then you will probably get in trouble too.

You know that you can recognize harm in its various forms. If a truck were coming at you, wouldn't you get out of the way? Of course you would. We need to look around and find out which of your friends or situations are like that truck. Then you need to get out of the way.

That crowd on the corner shooting craps is a potentially harmful situation. Illegal gambling with no real regulation can cause some tense situations. As soon as someone loses too much, or wins too much, there is going to be a problem.

That late night Chinese food joint, beer store, nuisance bars, and open-air drug markets are potential places for harm. Just look at the news and see how often shootouts occur there. You increase your chances of being caught in a crossfire when you hang out at these places.

Stay Ready – Get Ready

Jeff was a Boy Scout. I wasn't, but I always dug their motto: Be Prepared. Once my car broke down on the highway. To repair the simple problem with my carburetor, all that I needed was a screwdriver and a flashlight. I had neither. A bunch of cars passed me by. It was starting to snow, I had no cell phone, and it was starting to get dark.

I closed my eyes and said a quick prayer. A few minutes later, an old brother in an electrician's van pulled up and asked if I needed help. I told him about my problem and asked him if I could borrow a flashlight and a screwdriver.

He said he'd lend them to me, but that it would come with a lecture. He went on describing how he always keeps certain things in an emergency kit in his van. This was back in 1975, but the things he mentioned will still work today.

Here is what you need: get a box or a milk crate. Fill it with these basic tools – a flashlight, a flat screwdriver, a Phillips head screwdriver, a pair of pliers, an adjustable wrench, a tire gauge, a pair of jumper cables, a first-aid kit, road flares, a collapsible gas container, a blanket, some water, and a bag of candy or trail mix.

These are some of the basics that might get you by in the event of a breakdown.

Survival of the Fittest

For school, always have the books and supplies that you need. If you need books or supplies for class, have them in advance. Stay ready for anything, and you won't end up scrambling at the last minute.

Know Your Way Around

You should know at least three or four ways to get home from anywhere. You should know at least three or four ways to get to school or work.

If you catch the bus to work, make sure you know another bus line that can also get you there. What will you do if the bus company goes on strike? Do you have a bike? If it isn't too far, are you willing to walk? Do you have a friend or relative who will give you a ride? Are you willing to pay for gas?

When you drive, do you know another route to your usual destinations? Could you get to your school, job or court on time if the main roads were closed?

Can you read a map? Do you have a map of your local town or city? Can you plot a course to travel to another city? Can you locate any of the places that you hear about on the news on a national or world map?

If you can answer yes to all of the questions above, then you are ready. If not, then get some maps of your city, state, country and the world. Watch the news and try to find all of the places that made headlines. Before you know it, you will be geographically aware.

Always Eat Breakfast

As faculty members in predominantly African American schools, Jeff and I wonder aloud about our students' dietary habits. Many students come to school with a breakfast of chips and a soda. Some come with candy and sugary sweet drinks. This is no way to get your day started. Empty calories, like sugar, burn off quickly. Junk food won't last long enough to get you through a school or work day.

You need to eat some real food every morning. Breakfast is the most important meal of the day. Look at what your classmates eat in the morning. Those who eat candy and chips usually fall asleep before lunchtime. They have trouble concentrating after one or two classes. By their third period, their stomachs are growling, they have gas, or their minds are strictly on next period's lunch. You can't learn like that.

If you don't have enough to eat at home, then look into the school's free breakfast and lunch programs. Some young black people feel as if they are too good for the "freebie lunches." There is no shame in getting a free meal. We have seen students turn down a free meal, then complain that they are hungry an hour later. Only a fool turns down food when he is hungry.

Even if you only get to eat a bowl of cereal, you are giving yourself a fighting chance to survive the day. If you eat fruit, you give yourself the vitamins necessary to make your body work properly. So, don't skip breakfast.

If you look at older African American men, you will sere that a large number of them are diabetic or have high blood pressure. These problems don't develop overnight. They are the result of years of eating the wrong thing. It is a habit they formed when they were young men.

Educational
Survival

Learn How to Concentrate

You often hear about young people with attention deficit disorders and other problems that keep them from concentrating. Many young people who can't concentrate just have too many distractions.

On any given day, in many high schools across the country, you can look into classrooms and see the many distractions to concentrating. Kids talk on cell phones during class. Kids use computer time to access music videos. Kids are wearing MP-3's and I-Pods in their ears when they should be listening. All of these items can cause distractions in the wrong settings.

Don't bring radios, playing cards, dice, magazines, gum, or anything else that will take your mind off of your schoolwork. Don't bring old love letters, video games, pictures of relatives and pets, or rumors to class. All of these will keep you from learning. You can't learn your work while listening or looking at something else.

Concentrate on the work at hand by blocking out everything else and getting the job done. Put your cell phone on vibrate when you need to pay attention to something important. As a matter of fact, you don't need a phone in class at all. It will only distract you from your class work, which needs your complete concentration.

Don't Waste Your Time

A group called "The Last Poets" back in the '70's had a poem where they said that time was running out. They were right. Time is running out for young brothers who don't have their stuff together.

If you are standing on a corner, you are wasting valuable time that you could be using to advance your life. There is nothing that you can gain by standing on a corner.

If you are over 21 and you spend a lot of time playing video games, you are wasting time. Get off the couch and go live a real life.

If you spend your time watching T.V., videos, movies, cable, or surfing the web, check how much of your time is spent on these devices. Wasting too much time on these devices could take you away from interpersonal relationships. It also keeps you locked in a room while the rest of the world passes you by.

You can't get time back. Once it passes, it is gone. Use your youth wisely. Chase after your dreams and ideas while you are still young.

You make time your ally when you use it well. You make time your enemy when you waste it. The problem in our community is that brothers who waste time often end up doing time.

Pay Attention the First Time

Don't be one of those people who have to be told to do something over and over. All this does is make the person who is speaking mad.

If you are in a classroom and the teacher asks you to do something, don't sit there and make the teacher tell you more than once. This will affect your grade.

Don't make anyone in authority have to tell you something more than once because there are always consequences.

When the cops tell you to get out of a car, put your hands up, put your hands behind your back, or lay on the ground, don't wait to be told more than once. Your cooperation could be the difference between you getting hurt or not.

Don't have to be told twice to duck. You could lose your head. Don't have to be told twice to study. You could fail. Don't have to be told to leave people alone. You could face retaliation.

Pay attention and you won't have to be told anything more than once. People who only have to be told things once go farther in life than people who don't listen.

Travel As Often As Possible

Some people never leave their neighborhoods. Some are born, live their lives, and die without ever really going anywhere. Some folks don't leave their own little neighborhoods until the day they are carried out in a casket.

You find people who live in West Philly who have never been to North or South Philly. You have people in Brooklyn who have never been to the Bronx, Manhattan or Queens. You have people in South Central who have never been to Beverly Hills. You have people from the cities that have never been to the suburbs, and people in the suburbs who have never been to the city. It's really a shame.

If you stay in your own little box, you can never develop a wide view of the world. This is a big planet that we live on. The more you see, the more you will know. The more you know, the easier it is to survive in a world that treats black men as less than human.

Travel opens up new doors to understanding different people and cultures. Traveling to different countries will give you a chance to see how other people in the world solve their problems.

You can travel to some countries and find that you are treated better than you are in America. You can travel to countries that are ruled and governed by black people. You can travel to countries where their history did not include the African slave trade.

Even if you just travel to a different part of town, you are probably going to profit from the experience. You might find a restaurant that has something that you find delicious. You might find a store with some unique clothing. You might find a music store with that hard to get CD. You never know what you are going to find, but I guarantee you won't find anything sitting on your steps.

If You Don't Know, Ask

The nation's jails are full of people who claim they didn't know they were committing a crime. The judges chuckle when they tell you that ignorance is no excuse. The truth of the matter is that you know when you are doing something wrong.

You get a feeling in your gut when you know that you are doing the wrong thing. That is the moment when you make a decision. That is the moment that determines what is going to happen. If you have any doubts, then ask someone with common sense for advice.

If you think something might be illegal or immoral, seek the opinion of your parents, a teacher, your coach, or some other responsible adult. Don't ask your friends. They haven't been on the planet long enough to give you advice. Don't ask guys who get into trouble. They can't help you. Ask someone who is centered and taking care of himself and the lives of those around him.

Many times students tell us that they could not do their homework because they didn't really understand the work. The problem with that excuse is that they know they didn't understand the work during class. That's when they should have asked for help.

We meet young men who should have gone to college, who claim that they didn't know how to get money for tuition, so they didn't go. They should have asked everyone connected with the colleges that they wanted to attend. They should have asked other people who went to college. If you don't know, ask somebody.

Of course, not everyone is going to give you good advice. So, seek help from someone who has experienced what you want to experience.

The things you don't know <u>can</u> hurt you.

Uplift the Race

Be the Bling

"I am the Black gold of the sun," by Nuyorican Soul

Diamonds are created from coal. When the black lumps are put under pressure for a long time, the pressure turns the coal into bright, shining, beautiful gemstones. The challenges you face everyday are the things that forge your character. How you respond to those challenges move you down the path. Be wise and pick the path that leads to your best outcome.

Many young people get caught up in what they see the entertainers and athletes wearing and they all want to have ice dripping from their wrists and necks. I used to really hate that whole vibe until I saw photographs of a king and his court in a West African village and they were wearing more gold than the starting lineup of the NBA all-star teams. I'm still not into the bling bling, but I see it has roots. What I do love is the ability of our brothers to take the pressure of life and turn into the gemstones of the human race.

Be strong and let the pressure make you like a diamond: clear, bright, strong, and beautiful.

Have a Code of Conduct to Go Along with Your Belief System

Religion is important and African Americans have deep, abiding beliefs. In modern society, many faiths and belief systems are found among our people. Each belief system is held in reverence by believers. Proudly believe and use your faith to give you inner strength and divine guidance.

But even more importantly, for your survival, you must have and practice a code of conduct that you follow to keep yourself straight. If you operate within certain boundaries at home, in school, in the community, and in systems, you can enjoy yourself and minimize the risks you face.

So, have a firm grip on the things you will not do; use a gun or knife, use or deal narcotics or drugs, drink and drive, and so on. Every young man has many experiences he is anxious to try. Do it up. Go as many places and meet as many people as possible, but always keep it on the up and up, the positive side.

Have your own set of rules, but make sure they are rules that make sense and don't hurt yourself or others. Make sure that your rules are noble and have a sense of spiritual uplifting. Make sure that your rules honor the many black people who made it possible for you to be free.

Stay Off Shows that Humiliate Black People

If you want to see black people acting like fools, all you have to do is turn on the television. There are many daytime programs that seem intent on showing the most foolish black folks they can find.

On any given weekday, you can see Jerry Springer, Maury, Ricki Lake, Jenny Jones, and hosts of others that really make us look bad. You see baby-mama drama, deadbeat dads trying to escape paternity, partners who claim they didn't know that their lover was a man (or woman), confessions of adultery, cross-dressing, incest, prostitution, pimping, and fist-fighting.

Some people see this as just entertaining. The problem with these shows is that at least half or more of these wild guests are black. That is disturbing when we are only about 20% of the United States population. If only 20% of the people on these shows were black, then it might not be so glaringly racist.

People who aren't around African Americans see these shows and get the wrong impression of black people. It would be easy for someone from another country to think most black people are dysfunctional.

The directors of these shows must tell their talent scouts to find the worst looking, most foul-mouthed people they can find. Then they try to make you think that these are average people. No, they are sick people. Most don't need these talk shows. They need mental help.

The best thing you can do for yourself is not watch this type of junk. Find something worthwhile to do with your time. And never, ever, ever be tempted by any amount of money to appear on one of these shows.